Going Solo

Encouraging Single Catholics

Anne Stokes

En Route Books and Media, LLC
Saint Louis, MO

ENROUTE
Make the time

En Route Books and Media, LLC
5705 Rhodes Avenue
Saint Louis, MO 63109

Contact us at
contactus@enroutebooksandmedia.com

Cover credit: Photo by Giogio Trovato on Unsplash
Copyright 2025 Anne Stokes

ISBN-13: 979-8-88870-339-7
Library of Congress Control Number: 2025932136

All rights reserved. No part of this book may be reproduced, stored in a retrieval system, or transmitted in any form, or by any means, electronic, mechanical, photocopying, or otherwise, without the prior written permission of the author.

Table of Contents

Preface iii

Chapter One: A Solo-for-Life Story 1

Chapter Two: Single in the World: God's Perspective 15

Chapter Three: The Walls that Divide Us from God 27

Chapter Four: . . . And How to Keep Them Down 33

Chapter Five: Applied Theory or Practical Tips 47

Chapter Six: Speaking of Loneliness 57

Chapter Seven: Addressing Your Specific Status 71

Chapter Eight: Examples of Dedicated Single Persons ... 89

Chapter Nine: It Accumulates in "The End" 99

Preface

Every Sunday I am encouraged when our Deacon, prior to the celebration of the Holy Eucharist, prays what I call the "around-the-world" supplication that includes "Our Dedicated Single Persons." While the entire entreaty is special, it is that portion that reminds me that I am no more or less important to God than any of his other children. This prayer, coupled with my own journey, inspired me to write a work that would encourage single Catholics to follow in the footsteps of Jesus Christ.

Along with this prayerful and personal work, the focus will be on several aspects of life, including a scriptural understanding of God's will, and how to practically embrace it in a world that runs contrary to it. Since humanity's original fall from grace, we have tended to live in contradiction to our Father and Creator. His nature is pure and stable; our nature is impure and unstable. Consistently inconsistent, our moral compass whirls around in a state of flux from one generation to another. We are unable, without the help of God, to point consistently North, so to speak, hence we are often lost. With God, the direction is clear. Throughout all ages, places, and peoples - that have been or will be - it is in him that we are provided with changeless and dependable truth that gives meaning to this life. For in him, we find love, the joy of adoption, peace on earth, and eternal life.

Our Catholic faith is ancient in created time, yet eternal in God. Frequently considered out-of-date, like some fashion or perishable good, this conclusion is far from reality. Just as God is perfect, and his nature neither improves nor degrades, so it is with his good will for us. In him, the highest and best already exist, and that nature was exemplified in Jesus Christ who is eternally in vogue.

In a world that strives for, what seems to be, a never-ending need for improvement, we have a finished faith. We are told that what is new is better, and that change equals progress, yet with God, there is no need for such marketing tactics. God is who he is; changeless. The knowledge and beauty of this divine imagery is difficult at times to grasp because our flawed nature does not allow us to see with spiritual 20/20 vision. As the Apostle Paul said, "Now, we see through an unclear glass, later we shall see face-to-face. Now, I know partially, but later I shall know in full, as I am known in full." This imperfection of our mystical vision requires faith, for now. It is a faith, not founded upon myth, but grounded in the very life and precepts of Jesus Christ.

In this book, I have attempted to address several states of singleness, and though I am not experienced in all of them, the moral thread that ties them together is to be holy as God is holy. It is my hope that through Sacred Scripture, Church teaching, a few "been there done that" examples, and some practical suggestions that you may be encouraged to see the faith more clearly and practice it with confidence. Whether your current state is unwanted or embraced, may you find tools here-in that will assist you to become, or remain, in a dedicated "Solo" state.

Anne Stokes

Chapter One

A Solo-for-Life Story

From youth, I knew marriage and children were not for me.

~ Anne Stokes

When I was sixteen, I knew instinctively that I did not want to marry or have children. It is not something I can explain, it simply was what it was; a complete lack of desire. When the topic arose on "future" plans, often asked of young people, my response, "to remain single," was typically countered by, *You will change your mind when you get older.* When I was twenty-six, and asked similar questions, my reply was the same, but their response changed to, *You just haven't met the right person, yet.* By the age of thirty-six, the questions did not stop, but changed to the past tense, as in, *Do you have any children?* The questions themselves never bothered me; I knew it was a normal human inquiry. What was at times disconcerting was reading into their eyes, *Oh, you poor thing!*

When the time came to transition from high school to college, I began to question my conviction to never marry. Dating in high school had been, for me, a social activity not to be taken seriously. I never had a boyfriend because, frankly, I did not see the purpose. And with family, friends, church and studies, life was full and content. Attending college, however, I was confronted by several issues that would ultimately tear at the fabric of my personal conviction, and utterly shred my faith.

In high school, I told my parents I wanted to be a missionary, so with their blessings I enrolled as a missions major at a bible college affiliated with my denomination. When I arrived at school my excitement co-mingled with other like-minded freshmen who were going to bring Christ to the darkest regions of the world. Being the daughter of a pastor, I had been exposed to many foreign missionaries and admired them so much that, becoming a missionary was my only vocational dream. Yet, by the end of my freshman year that dream began to fade as one spiritual wave after another rocked my "hope" boat. For it was in that first year that I began to hesitate about foreign missions work, not from the work itself, but because I discovered an officially *unofficial* prerequisite to becoming a missionary; what I call "wave number one."

Wave Number One: *Single women need not apply.*

The idea of marriage was never pushed on me by my parents, though it remained a "hope," along with grandchildren. They knew how I felt about the topic. Neither did they discourage me from becoming a single missionary, so you may imagine my surprise when I learned the missions program assumed marriage prior to serving. In fact, the anecdote on campus was that women only attended to get their M.R.S. degree! In addition, it was the men who studied theology, Hebrew and Greek, while the women were expected to learn the piano, teach children, and support their husband. This was pressed home when I took Koine Greek, and as the only female in the class became something of a joke on campus. Though doubt regarding my chosen field began to seep in, I continued into my sophomore year where two more waves hit my boat.

Wave Number Two: *I have a crush, but on my room-mate.*

In the fall of 1981, I entered into my sophomore year with the same room-mate from the year prior. We got along great, and I liked her, but so much so that I did not enjoy seeing her husband-hunting. This first-time feeling toward a woman was confusing. Was it just a harmless "crush," or was it something more? Honestly, I had no clue. Entering college a virgin, and completely inexperienced with romance, let alone sex, my fondness for her bewildered me. And I should point out that in 1981 it was not a good time to explore, even theoretically, such perplexity. Aside from being a potential sin, which I was aware that homosexuality was, that same year the Moral Majority was in full swing, and my school supported it militantly. The E.R.A. movement, feminism, and homosexuality were hot, if not hostile, topics of the lips of preachers as well as ordinary folks. It was not uncommon to read, "Adam and Eve, not Adam and Steve," on the bumper sticker of a car back then, and few public figures were "out of the closet." For some, it was a matter of privacy, yet for others, their very livelihoods depended upon discretion. This was the state of the world at the time of my dilemma, and I contemplated what to do. Do I speak with a counselor? Call my parents? Or do I keep it inside my mental closet. The latter seemed most appropriate, and though I kept it to myself, I did speak openly with one person: God.

As the feelings for my roommate lingered, I asked God, "Where is all this coming from, and why me?" An "A" student academically, I was marking off all the wrong boxes on the Christian exam of life. Marriage-minded? *No*. Children? *No*. Sexual Orientation? *Undetermined*. Plagued by doubt and disillusionment, my grades began to falter, my mood changed, and for the first time in my life I began to experience a sense of isolation. As I cried out to the Lord, even he seemed deaf to my prayers. Like an echo bouncing back from a large canyon, my "whys?" only returned unanswered.

Wave Number Three: *Is there a God?*

By the end of my sophomore year, my spiritual foundation was crumbling. The Baptist faith in which I was raised was the first to fall to scrutiny, and after that, came Christianity and God. The storm that spawned this fresh wave came in the form of a college course in Church History. By no means a scholar at that point, numerous red flags were raised and there was something not quite right with the Baptist version being taught.[1] As the wave of questions rolled in with greater and greater force, the doubts mounted, and along with the doubts, my approach to God - the only person in whom I confided - changed. I stopped asking him *why* and began to accuse him of making me different. *What had I done to deserve all this uncertainty?!* I had been a good kid, followed all the rules, and never questioned anything before, so this cannot possibly be my fault.

Convinced of his unfairness, I began to pull away from God. My hereditary faith, my life boat, had become seriously damaged from a constant set of waves striking it. Within two short years I had transformed from a happy and optimistic Christian to a miserable agnostic, and the change was perceptible. I breathed sarcasm and negativity to the point that other students noticed, and I could no longer stand myself. During Christmas break of my junior year, I dropped

---

[1] This is covered more in my book, *Will the Real Church Please Stand!* (En Route Books and Media, 2023)

Chapter One: A Solo-for-Life Story

out of school and returned home. If there had been a God, he would never have allowed all this to happen to me.

Wave Number Four: *Deep Waters*

Returning home, I hid my attitude and agnosticism as best I could for the sake of my parents. It was a fruitless endeavor, for they could see that my personality had changed and had no clue as to why. Their perplexity only added to my pain; I loved my parents deeply, and knew full well that none of this was their fault, yet what could I say? How could I begin to express years of angst and dread that might only hurt them. Isolated and backed into a corner by my own hand, I convinced myself that I was now a lousy daughter, and that my parents deserved better. Within a few weeks of returning home, this last dark wave hit my sinking boat, and it capsized. The questions and doubts had become irrelevant, and I allowed myself to be swept out to sea through an attempted suicide. I did not want to give in. I did not want to die. I simply could not tolerate the spiritual and mental beating any longer.

***

Obviously, I did not succeed in my attempt, yet surviving did not immediately change my outlook. If anything, my perspective on life had shifted into neutral. Neither moving forward, nor backward, I existed. My parents arranged for counseling, which helped me to not go into reverse; but little more. After a few months of aimless floating, I finally decided to try and move forward, even if that meant embracing an uncertain future. Taking a full-time job and enrolling in night classes at a state university, I was able to transfer away from home and the concerning eyes of my parents. Still an agnostic, the feeling of former dread was replaced with a spiritual numbness of no longer caring. As time passed, however, the desire for answers began to resurface, and my naturally inquisitive mind began looking into all those unanswered questions. This time though, I would not look for answers within the context of Christianity, but the world that I now embraced. For it was in the world that I found initial acceptance, and where, at the very least, a place that did not view my concerns as abnormal. And with secular times changing quickly, particularly in California, I found that both work and university offered a safe environment for exploration. It was common to doubt, or even deny, the existence of God. It was also not uncommon to be sexually curious. In addition, my initial desire to remain unmarried and childless would prove to be boost later on as I climbed the corporate ladder. All in all, the world provided a liberation from prior constraints, and I thrived on that liberty for over two decades. Throwing off the yoke of Christianity had been the best thing for my self-esteem, as I became a normal person in a normal world doing normal things, and best of all, I was moving forward.

The End?

Not quite.

I may have forgotten about God, but he had not forgotten about me.

During those twenty years, I found answers to my questions, and in theory, I even concluded there was a God, and that Christianity was the highest and best form of faith; yet I remained non-practicing. There was still a deep-seated resentment toward God, and I no longer believed Baptists were the "true" New Testament Church they claimed to be. There was also a great blessing that occurred during that time, and that was a closer relationship with my parents.

Despite my chosen life-style, we evolved from a simple parent-child relationship to one of best friends, and it would be this bond of love that God would use as a catalyst for change.

When I was forty-three, my father died. Four long years he suffered with cancer, and we suffered with him. In spite of the pain, his faith did not falter; and it was a bold faith. Since I was a child, my father had a penchant for clinging to God's promises and reminding him of them, too! Without hesitation he would say, "God, you promised..." while praying. Both he and my mother held the strong belief that God kept his word. One promise of God they claimed for their children was Proverbs 22:6, "Train up a child in the way they should go, and when they are old, they will not depart from it." Rather than try and fix something first, they would turn to God, especially for things they could not control – like an adult child. And though my father did not live to see me return to the fold, I know he died *believing* in that promise, and he would shortly be proven right.

Several months after his funeral, I was browsing a bookstore and while rummaging in the discount stack my eyes caught the title, *The Purpose Driven Life*. I had heard of the book and was familiar with

Chapter One: A Solo-for-Life Story

the author, Rick Warren, who pastored an evangelical mega-church near my home. Scanning the cover that read "over 15 million copies sold" I thought it might be interesting, so I bought it. Little did I know that somewhere in that ordinary moment God was working in an extraordinary way.

The next day, as I sat in my kitchen drinking coffee, I began to read the book and to my surprise, by the fifth chapter little tears formed in my eyes. What I was reading made me think of a verse I had not read in a very long time; "Choose today whom you will serve." It was from the Old Testament Book of Joshua. I knew the story behind the verse, and in that moment, I was confronted by yet another question; would I continue on my chosen path, or return to the God of my childhood?

The Sunday following, I began attending an evangelical church near my home where, in the weeks to come, the back pew became my "spot." As I listened to the word and sang, or tried to sing, the old familiar hymns, I could not help but weep, hence the back row seating. First came a sense of shame, then remorse, and finally, gratitude. It was twelve months of introspection mingled with joy and sorrow before I could even touch the bread and wine offered each month.

My life had mirrored the prodigal son Jesus spoke of in Luke 15:11-32. And though my awakening was not so extreme, the full weight of how I had lived in willful disobedience crushed my heart.

That first church service was now two decades ago, nearly the same amount of time I had lived in disobedience. There were some hiccups early on, for the last thing the flesh, world, and devil want is to see a lost sheep return to the fold. Even still, nothing has stood between myself, God, and the desire to live a fully committed single life in Christ.

Change, *true* change, may take several attempts because the pleasures of this world are addictive. They are easy to start, difficult to stop, yet worth the struggle to free oneself from the bondage; and sin is binding. For twenty years, I fooled myself into thinking that Christianity was the "ball and chain" that kept me from being who I was naturally, and that *this* world offered freedom; I was wrong. Real liberty comes with Christ. Wonderful for a time, even for a wayward Christian, the pleasures of this world are not meant to satisfy. For beneath the dazzling surface of sinful pleasure there is an ulterior motive that encourages disobedience to God. Not everything that appears to be good, is good.

Chapter One: A Solo-for-Life Story

If you are struggling today with some form of disobedience, never give up the fight to obey. Life is not easy, and the Apostle Paul taught us that *perseverance* in the faith is key. We stumble, yet we get up again. As C.S. Lewis profoundly put it:

> No amount of falls will really undo us if we keep picking ourselves up each time. We shall of course be very muddy and tattered children by the time we reach home. But the bathrooms are all ready, the towels put out, and the clean clothes are in the airing cupboard. The only fatal thing is to lose one's temper and give it up. It is when we notice the dirt that God is most present in us; it is the very sign of His presence.

Chapter Two

Single in the World: God's Perspective

I no longer call you servants, because a servant does not know his master's business. Instead, I have called you friends, for everything that I learned from my Father I have made known to you.

~ John 15:15

Have you ever wondered why God did not create Adam and Eve at the same time? I do not claim to know the mind of God, but it appears to me that maybe God would have been perfectly happy with a single human being. He knew, of course, that he would create a companion for Adam, yet the question remains. Whatever God intended, he came to see that in creating Adam, Adam was alone in his uniqueness and fully aware of it. God, therefore, who is infinite in love, created Eve, a being of Adam's own kind for companionship.

Perhaps you are like Adam and feel uniquely alone. Or, perhaps you are single like me and enjoy it. It is not "how we feel," or even "how we got here," that binds us together, but the fact that we are Catholics seeking to please God. Whatever the reason may be, being single is a challenge, and that challenge is no less exacerbated by the world in which we live. For it says one thing, when God says another. To seek the right path, when there are so many available, is possible, *if we so choose*. And the choice behind the freedom is best understood from God's perspective.

What does God think about Us as Individuals?

This question alone should inspire awe, or least a moment of pause, that God thinks of you – specifically. Here we are, on a planet with billions of people, and God knows the very number of hairs on our collective heads![2] Why such minute detail? Because every part of us is precious to God our father.

---

[2] Luke 12:7, "Even the hairs on your head are counted. So don't be afraid! You are worth much more than many sparrows."

Chapter Two: Single in the World: God's Perspective

When I was a little girl, my dad used to say that I was the "apple of his eye," which made no sense to me at the time. Only later did I learn that it was a phrase of endearment. I was precious to him. The phrase itself comes from an old English translation of Psalms 17:8, where King David asks God to "Keep me as the apple (i.e. pupil) of your eye, hide me under the shadow of your wings." And Jesus used the latter part of this phrase when, in speaking as God to the Jews, he compared himself to a mother hen, saying,

> Jerusalem, Jerusalem, you who kill the prophets and stone those sent to you, how often I have longed to gather your children together, as a hen gathers her chicks under her wings, and you were not willing.

God's love toward us is no less than that of a mother hen or bear protecting her cubs. Three ways in which he has revealed this great love toward us are by his demonstrating good intentions, his revealing flawless wisdom, and his giving us a free will.

God the Father is 100% good and only intends good for his children. He is neither a mythical old man "upstairs" who delights in seeing your fun spoiled, nor is he an overly permissive parent who cares more about your friendship than your welfare. God, as our heavenly father, is the perfect balance of what parenthood should be, loving and authoritative with only the best intentions. Most of us get a glimpse of this, if imperfect, through our earthly parents.

One of the first experiences of parental "good intentions" that I recall came in the form of my mother, who was the chief disciplinarian in the family. As a child, I recall grocery shopping with her and asking for some sugary cereal (I think it was *Count Chocula*), and hearing her say, "No, it's not good for you," while she reached for the oh-so-boring *Corn Flakes*. I had no idea what she meant by it "not being good for me" because everyone at school was eating it, so I simply concluded that she was just unfair. As I matured, however, I began to understand that her intention was not to treat me unfairly, but to guide me toward good health. It is like this with God, for his knowledge and wisdom is magnified by perfection.

God's wisdom, which is flawless, does us little good if he keeps it to himself. When God communicated his will toward us, what is called "revelation," that is to say, he pulled open a curtain to reveal the light, his revealing came in the form of his spoken word, that was later written. The revealing of his will came in two steps. First, he conveyed a rule, such as *Thou shall not...*, and later, after the people began to mature, he explained the reason for his rule. Like little children who must first learn to obey without question, because they are unable to understand that running into the street can be fatal, we too learn by obedience before we are able to grow into spiritual maturity. As God, he certainly does not have to explain himself, yet he desires for us to grow up in both knowledge and understanding.

In several ways spiritual growth is analogous to physical. We fuel our bodies first with soft food, then solid, and as we mature over time, our ability to reason begins to form. Likewise, as we grow spiritually, we should begin to mature beyond the simple foods of the faith, or what the apostle Paul called "milk," and comprehend more deeply God and his precepts. God no more desires a 30-year-old spiritual baby than a mother would want to bottle-feed an adult child. We are created for growth, and as we evolve, God's will toward us expands to incorporate more expectations.

Assuming that we are no longer eating divine baby food, God moves beyond the "Do as I say," to

"Do as I say, *because*..." in order that we may understand. For example, God commanded in the Old Testament that we live a chaste life until we are married, and in the New Testament he further revealed why. For example, in I Corinthians 6:13-20 the apostle Paul states - and here I am paraphrasing – the reason behind the command to be chaste.

> ...the body is not designed for sexual sin, but for the Lord, and we should flee all fornication because sexual immorality is a sin against our body, which is the temple of the Holy Spirit, and our body is no longer ours to do with as we please.

The command is chastity; the reason is because our body is the temple of the Holy Spirit. In becoming God's child, we no longer "own" our body, but are expected to treat it with respect.

God has freely given to us, and he desires us to freely respond, which is why he provided humanity with a free will. God did not create rational beings for companionship, but to be known, and freely loved. In Genesis it says he created humans in his likeness to take charge over the earth and to reflect him, for as infinite Spirit, he cannot be known to his creation in essence, as "no one has ever seen God." He cannot be totally grasped, but his likeness can be. In addition, scripture tells us that God wants us to know him and to love him, for it says, "Let him who glories glory in this – that he understands and knows ME," and also "To love him with all our heart, soul and mind." Basically, God desires a personal relationship with us, yet one that is not forced, but voluntary.

My father, who was a Baptist pastor, in stressing the idea of voluntary love from the pulpit, would often say, "Isn't it better when your child comes running up to you and says 'Daddy, I love you!' than for you to command, "Come here and tell me you love me." Love freely given is more precious than if it were demanded.

Coupled with our ability to reason, we have been given, as mentioned, a voluntary nature, that is to say the ability to act or not act according to our own will. Our "free will" is key to a personal relationship with God because he desires us to love him *voluntarily*. How we show that voluntary love will be covered in Chapter Four; and you may be surprised that it is not the same as humans show to each other.

What does God think of this world?

It may seem illogical that scripture reveals, "God so loved the world that he gave his only Son," and yet "hates" this world at the same time. He actually refers to it as his enemy, and those who love it, his enemy as well.[3] This seeming paradox, something which GK Chesterton would have enjoyed, is easily remedied when put into proper context.

In *loving* the world, God meant his creation, which he called "good."[4] After Adam and Eve fell from grace, however, that good was interrupted by sin, that resulted in death; both physical and spiritual. Sin placed an abyss between us and God, and yet, because of his love, God did not give up on us. The ultimate proof of this was manifested through the life, death, and resurrection of Jesus Christ, "that *whoever* believes in him will not perish, but have everlasting life."

---

[3] James 4:4, "...don't you know that being a friend of the world pits you against God? Whoever, therefore, is a friend of the world is the enemy of God."

[4] In Genesis 1:12-25, we read several times the phrase, "and God saw that it was good," mentioned after his creative acts.

Chapter Two: Single in the World: God's Perspective 23

In *hating* the world, God is referring to the spiritually dark realm inhabited by all the created forces that have rejected him. The first rejection was that of Lucifer and his rebellious angels, and the second was manifested in Adam and Eve's disobedience. The "world," therefore, refers to a very real space in time that is associated with our beautiful planet, but is not our planet. He loves his creation, but he hates the spiritually dark choices that rational creatures have made against him through disobedience. This is why, as you will read later on, obedience means so much to God that he equates it with love. Now, this spiritual darkness which cannot dwell in heaven, is, for the time being, limited to created space, and thus it cloaks our earth with its putrid air.

After his fall from heaven,[5] Satan was banished from heaven to earth, which became his temporary home and where he now rules as the "prince of the power of the air,"[6] working behind the scenes, so to

---

[5] See Isaiah 14:12–14 and Ezekiel 28:12–18 regarding the fall of Satan, and also Luke 10:18 for what Jesus has to say about him.

[6] Ephesians 2:2.

speak, with his fallen angels.[7] Just beneath the surface of physical creation there is a hostile reality, "not made with flesh and blood," that seeks to destroy God and all that is good. One way in which Satan seeks to destroy what is good is to detract from the worship of God. Satan would prefer all creation to worship him, but in the end, he is satisfied as long as God is not obeyed or adored. We see Satan's claim to temporal rulership and the desire to be worshipped clearly when he tempts Jesus during his forty days of fasting.

Toward the end of his fasting, Satan took Jesus up to the peak of a mountain and showed him all the kingdoms of the world, and said, "All this I will give you, if you bow down and worship me."[8] This was perhaps one time that Satan spoke the truth, for it was in his power to give earthly kingdoms, but his motive was sin. God calls Satan the "father of lies," and the apostle Paul describes him as the "spirit that works in people to disobey." It is this spiritually dark world, the

---

[7] We do not know how many angels followed Lucifer in his rebellion, but in Revelation 12, it suggests a number of one-third. Again, one-third of what, we do not know, yet they appeared as "stars" that plunged from heaven to earth.

[8] Matthew 4:8-9.

one that entices us to disobey, that has become God's enemy. But God, in his love, encourages us to "Not copy the behavior and customs of this world, but be a new and different person by transforming your mind."[9] Our life is literally a spiritual tug-of-war between heaven and hell.

Back in the 1970s, the phrase "The devil made me do it!" was popularized by the comedian Flip Wilson. His skit was funny, as was he, yet as Christians we know that the devil, as powerful as he is, cannot force us to disobey. Being created with a free will means that neither God nor Satan may coerce us into *anything*. God desires good, and Satan may tempt, but the accountability for our voluntary actions rests solely on us.

---

[9] Romans 12:2.

Chapter Three

The Walls that Divide Us from God

"But your iniquities have separated you from your God; your sins have hidden his face from you, so that he will not hear."

~ *Isaiah 59:2*

Walls are meant for one purpose: to divide. In 1990, I visited Berlin with friends and one of our first stops was to see the remains of the infamous Berlin Wall. It was built in 1961 by communist East Germany to keep their people in, and other people out. It literally divided a once unified German populace into the free and the non-free. From the Great Wall of China to the legal segregation of races in American history, walls of some sort have been built to separate. Ironically, of all the things God created, walls were not among them. In the Garden of Eden, there were no walls, as created life roamed freely. God had no reason for division, for in him, peace reigned. Barriers are the by-product of sin, an original contribution of the rational being. With human beings, there are many ideas associated with the word "sin" that miss the point. There are dozens of witticisms regarding sin and sinners, and at least one city jokingly referred to as "Sin City." With God, however, sin is no laughing matter.

Simply put, biblical sin is voluntary *disobedience* to a known law of God. The English word "sin" comes from the Greek *hamartia* (ἁμαρτία), and depending upon the context, it describes an act or attitude of lawlessness, spiritual anarchy, or defiance. The ability to commit sin is an exclusive, and inherent, trait in the free will being.

While the first recorded sin we know of was that of Lucifer rebelling against God, humanly speaking, it was Adam and Eve who got the ball rolling. Acting as a unified whole, both chose to disobey God's one rule: "Don't eat the fruit from that specific tree." When they defied God and ate the fruit, a spiritual wall was raised between their sin and their sinless Creator.

This first wall, referred to theologically as "original sin," eternally separated them, and all humanity thereafter, from God. I say, *eternally*, because, without the help of God, they had no power to undo what they had done. Like a word that escapes the lips can never be unspoken, they had built a wall they could not tear down. It was God, who in his love and mercy, produced a way for reconciling their broken relationship with him, and that way came in the form of a very high price, bloodshed.

The Necessity for Bloodshed

For some nonbelievers, and those who do not understand, the necessity of shedding blood is a repulsive aspect of salvation history. I have heard it said that the Christian focus on blood is morbid, and on the surface, it is; even to God. Yet there is a good reason behind the requirement.

In the story of Adam and Eve, their sin of disobedience necessitated the shedding of blood, for we are told that God provided them "coats of skin," to cover their sin and allow them to remain in union with him. Prior to this act of rebellion, no living creature was ever slain. And later, when God selected Abraham to be the father of his chosen people (the Hebrews), he tested Abraham's faith and obedience by ordering him to sacrifice his beloved son Isaac.[10] Centuries later, when Moses rescued the Hebrews from Egypt, God gave Moses laws for his people. Among them were laws pertaining to animal sacrifices that were required for the forgiveness of sin. The author of the Book of Hebrews, in writing on blood, wrote, "…the law requires that nearly everything be cleansed with blood, and without the shedding of blood there is no forgiveness." Now, one might ask and rightfully so, why was bloodshed required for forgiveness? It is because, only in the taking of life could God, the Author of Life, instill in his people the gravity of disobedience. Sin is equated with *death*, as the scriptures say, "The wages [or penalty] of sin is death." And as sin is death, that nourishing red liquid that runs through the body is equated with *life*. As death conquered life, so must life conquer death, and God required that the life's blood be shed in exchange for death caused by sin. It was not God who created sin or death, but we who have a free will that first manifested sin toward him.

---

[10] Isaac, of course, was not slain, and through him came Jacob, and the Twelve Tribes of Israel that Moses would later rescue out of Egypt.

God never wanted blood sacrifice,[11] yet this costly *quid pro quo* demand taught the people how deadly serious sin is. And the gravity of the penalty came to a climax with the sacrifice of Jesus Christ on the cross. The animal "sin offerings" under the Law of Moses, which had to be repeated, prefigured the ultimate and final sacrifice of Jesus Christ; the perfect "Lamb" of God.

Today, with the fulfillment of the Old Testament prophecies through the obedience of Jesus the Messiah, we are able to have our original sin washed away in the waters of Baptism. This sacramental rite, that symbolizes the death, burial, and resurrection of Jesus Christ, broke down the *first* wall of sin that Adam and Eve passed on to humanity. As the Church teaches,

> Baptism, by imparting the life of Christ's grace, erases original sin and turns a man back toward God, but the consequences for [our] nature, weakened and inclined to evil,

---

[11] 1 Samuel 15:22: "To obey, is better than sacrifice."

persist in man and summon him to spiritual battle.[12]

This is great news, though it does not automatically keep us from building our own walls of sin.

Personal sins, those we alone commit, erect fresh walls between us and God. Baptism wiped away original sin, but when we commit further sins against God, they too must be washed away if we are to remain in union with him. This cleansing is done through repentance and confession. The purpose of the Rite of Reconciliation is to obtain forgiveness with the intent to "go and sin no more," and by doing so we maintain our relationship with God. Still, it is important to keep in mind that God would prefer we obey, *first*, rather than seek absolution after the fact.

***

In the next chapter, the focus will be three ways in which God has provided for us to avoid building walls of sin. Each stage will build on the other and is based on Sacred Scripture and Tradition.

---

[12]*Catechism of the Catholic Church*, 405.

Chapter Four

...*And How to Keep Them Down*

Start by doing what is necessary, then what is possible, and suddenly you are doing the impossible.

~ St. Francis of Assisi

Just as obedience is better than sacrifice, stopping a wall of sin from building up between us and God is better than tearing it down later. In order to be proactive in this sense, we need something called spiritual discernment.

Spiritual discernment is foresight based on wisdom and knowledge. It is not acquired overnight but develops in stages. Like the quote above from St. Francis, which I will use as a template, the ability to discern begins first with what is necessary (obedience), then what is possible (informed faith in action), and finally, what is impossible (developing the mind of Christ).

Stage 1

Start by doing what is necessary: obedience.

This first step is so simple that a child can do it; but simple is not always easy! An unwillingness to obey comes with our fallen nature. We encounter this in everyday life when we see, for example, that children do not naturally want to "share" their toys. As adults, we recognize that selfish behavior is socially unacceptable and therefore teach children at a young age to not hog all the toys. Our tendency toward self-centeredness requires correction, and that process normally begins with positive negativity.

Children, even babies, quickly learn that "No!" is something negative. Yet what appears as negative to them is later understood to have been positively motivated. An older child will realize that there is a very good reason why Mom said "No!" when they crawled toward the cat's food. Likewise, as new Christians we begin as children in the faith. We must begin obeying the seemingly negative commands of God, until we understand why God says, "No!" And learning obedience is the first step in loving God.

God equates obedience with love.

When it comes to love, it is natural for humans to show it in several ways. A kiss, a hug, or even a flower may indicate our love for another. With God, it is not the same. And if we are to love him, as he desires for us to, then we need to look at love from his perspective.

God is spirit, and wholly different from his creation in essence. Though God is not emotionless, *per se,* his desires are not anthropomorphic. He cannot be hugged or kissed or even handed a flower. Therefore, to properly show our love for him we must offer him what he equates to love, and that is obedience to his will. Jesus expressed this divine definition of love when he said, "If you love me, you will keep my commandments." Now, you may think that obedience is just cold-hearted duty, and where is the love in that? The love is not the act itself but stems from our *desire* to obey. That desire, to please God, shows him our love. And that love was perfected in the obedient life of Christ.

One of my most cherished devotionals is *The Imitation of Christ* by Thomas à Kempis. This work, written in the 15th century, speaks to the very love that God would have us give him; a life of obedience like that of his beloved Son. And what does that obedient life look like? In a nutshell, Jesus expressed it himself saying:

> *If any of you wants to be my follower, you must put aside your own pleasures and shoulder your cross, and follow me closely. If you insist on saving your life (i.e. doing things your way), you will lose it. Only those who disregard their lives for my sake and for the sake of the Good News will ever know what it means to really live.*[13]

To love God, as he desires, is to willfully pattern our life after the life of his Son, Jesus Christ.

---

[13] Mark 8:34-36.

Stage 2

Then what is possible: an informed faith in action.

What begins with obedience leads to the next step of developing an informed faith in action. Just as children are encouraged to "grow up" and become responsible adults, God also wants us to be established in our faith. This is accomplished by moving away from divine baby food (e.g. simple truths), to feeding on solid food for a deeper understanding. This is exactly what Jesus did with his disciples. During his ministry, Jesus took simple fishermen and matured their faith by his word and example.

Our faith was never meant to remain elementary, but to be transformed to a higher level through greater knowledge of Sacred Scripture. Think of faith as a flashlight. A simple faith is a flashlight with dead batteries, whereas an informed faith is fully charged. Only an informed faith provides the ability to spiritually see in a dark world, discern good from bad, and maneuver along that narrow road Jesus spoke of.[14]

---

[14] Matt. 7:13-14, "Enter through the narrow gate. For wide is the gate and broad is the road that leads to

Prior to his ascension into heaven, Jesus prayed two prayers to the Father in heaven. One for his immediate disciples and one for those who would later believe (i.e. us). Excerpts of his prayers are below. Read it carefully (words bolded are mine for emphasis):

For My Disciples

> *I have revealed you to those whom you gave me out of the world. They were yours; you gave them to me and **they have obeyed your word**. Now **they know** that everything you have given me comes from you.*
>
> *I am not praying for the world, but for those you have given me, for they are yours.*
>
> *I will remain in the world no longer, but they are still in the world, and I am coming to you.*

---

destruction, and many enter through it. But small is the gate and narrow the road that leads to life, and only a few find it."

Chapter Four: ...And How to Keep Them Down

> *Holy Father, protect them by the power of your name, the name you gave me, so that they may be one as we are one.*
>
> *I have given them your word and the world has hated them, for **they are not of the world any more than I am of the world.***
>
> *My prayer is not that you take them out of the world but that you protect them from the evil one.*
>
> *Sanctify them by the truth; **your word is truth**.*
>
> ***As you sent me into the world, I have sent them into the world.***

Immediately after this, Jesus prays for all believers;

> *My prayer is not for them [the disciples] alone.*
>
> *I **pray also for those who will believe in me through their message**, that all of them*

> *may be one, Father, just as you are in me and I am in you.*
>
> *May they also be in us so **that the world may believe** that you have sent me.*

In these prayers, Jesus mentions obedience and informed faith, but he also includes one more thing: *action*. Going back to the flashlight analogy, even a fully charged light (i.e., intellectual faith) is useless if it is not switched on. An informed faith is activated by doing what Saint James called "works." In writing about obedience, faith and works in his book,[15] he conveys to us the same formula that Jesus taught him and the disciples: Obedience + Informed Faith + Action = God's will. James wrote that, "faith without works is dead." By this he means that works (that outward evidence of an inward faith) bring our intellectual faith to life for others to see. We would call it today, "walking the talk." This is exactly what God desires for us to do, to be lights reflecting him in this

---

[15] The Book of James is brief with just five chapters, but in those few pages there is an abundance of wisdom for practical Christian living.

spiritually dark world. And when we walk our talk, we are ready for the impossible.

Stage 3

Doing the impossible: obtaining the mind of Christ.

After tackling obedience and activating an informed faith, the last stage in our sequence is to develop the mind of Christ. For only in thinking like Christ may we truly begin to imitate him and thus show our love toward God. This stage has two components: mind and body.

<u>Our Mind</u>

The apostle Paul, that great missionary and disciple of Jesus, wrote to the church at Phillipi, "Let this mind be in you, which was also in Christ Jesus." What Paul was alluding to was Christ's attitude of humility and selflessness: two traits that do not come naturally to us. Prone to pride and greed, obtaining the mind of Christ requires time, effort, and a good deal of unlearning what our old nature tells us, and learning what our new nature requires. Beginning with obedience and an informed faith is a great start, but the battle of the natures has now begun.

Born with a sinful nature opposed to God, we are spiritually "reborn" in the regenerative waters of Baptism. This rebirth gives us a new nature, not grounded in sin, but in Christ. By the power of the Holy Spirit, we are then enabled to break the bonds of sin, or to "just say no" to temptation – as Christ did. The challenge, that Christ did not have, is dealing with both natures at the same time!

In 1984, Pat Benatar released a hit single entitled "Love is a Battlefield." That describes the war between our two natures perfectly. The old sinful nature does not want to give up any territory to the new, and a battle between love of self and love of God begins.

The apostle Paul, in his second letter to the church at Corinth, says that between our old and new natures there exists a spiritual "war of the mind," for he says, "… the weapons of our warfare are not physical," and that only spiritual weapons will pull down the strongholds of temptation. Jesus provided a perfect example of spiritual warfare when he used Sacred Scripture against the temptations of Satan in the wilderness.

It is contrary to our natural instinct to protect ourselves through invisible means. We want real shields and swords that we can relate to, but in spiritual battle, we are only able to "cast down imaginations and every high thing that exalts itself against the knowledge of God" with spiritual weapons. What are these weapons? They are described in Ephesians 6:10-20, where the Apostle Paul uses the analogy of a real soldier in his day. Along with prayer and an alert mind, Paul said we are to arm ourselves with the belt of *truth*, breastplate of *righteousness*, helmet of *salvation*, shield of *faith* and the sword of the Spirit, which is *Sacred Scripture*. These prepare us for spiritual battle against God's enemies, and especially Satan.

Our Body

The two natures dueling for superiority of our mind are contained within our one original body. This body, which scripture sometimes calls "the flesh," is not regenerated with our new nature, in fact, it tends to cling to the old one! The body as biblical *flesh*, is part of the triune enemy of God, commonly phrased "the world, the flesh and the devil."[16] Because the flesh (and its desires) does not become our friend immediately upon baptism, it takes training to align it with our new nature. The flesh, particularly our sensory organs are the gateways to the mind, and controlling them is one way of protecting our new nature.

Have you ever heard of *Garbage In, Garbage Out*, or the phrase *You are what you eat*? Both of these refer to the necessity of correct input for correct results. These adages also apply spiritually-speaking. In the same way that poor data entered into a computer results in poor output, our mind is able to intake unhealthy sights and sounds that result in harm to our mental health. Like the children's song that goes, "Be careful little eyes what you see," it is our responsibility to ensure only good input, and we do this by applying

---

[16] The phrase is not explicitly stated in Sacred Scripture, but the context is implied in I John 2:15-17, which reads, "Do not love the world or anything in the world. If anyone loves the world, love for the Father is not in them. For everything in the world—the lust of the flesh, the lust of the eyes, and the pride of life, comes not from the Father but from the world. The world and its desires pass away, but whoever does the will of God lives forever."

Chapter Four: ...And How to Keep Them Down

the filter of spiritual discernment mentioned above. This is particularly important when it comes to immorality. As new creations in Christ, our body is no longer ours alone, but the dwelling place of the Holy Spirit. Our body is to treat our new nature like a temple. In writing on this topic, the apostle Paul told the church at Corinth:

> Flee from sexual immorality. Every other sin a man can commit is outside his body, but he who sins sexually sins against his own body. Do you not know that your body is a temple of the Holy Spirit who is in you, whom you have received from God? You are not your own; you were bought at a price. Therefore glorify God with your body.[17]

To have the mind of Christ, therefore, is to have self-control of both mind and body. God does not expect us to be perfectly sinless, but he wants us to work toward that goal of imitating the sinlessness of Jesus.

As I close out this chapter, and we head into some practical tips, I would like to take a moment to cover

---

[17] I Corinthians 6:18-20.

a few things that made Jesus special as a perfect human example. Jesus Christ, our Creator God, chose to live in a human body and to be placed temporarily "a little lower than the angels." In obedience to the Father, he took on this humble role, but (and this is just like Jesus) he went even further in the humility category. Consider the following.

1. He was homeless and without worldly possessions,[18]
2. He lived without societal status,[19]
3. He was abused by his own creation,[20] and finally,
4. He gave his life as a sacrifice for our sins, in voluntary obedience.[21]

---

[18] Matthew 8:20.
[19] John 1:46.
[20] Luke 22:63-23:12.
[21] Philippians 2:8.

Chapter Five

Applied Theory or Practical Tips

The greatest danger for most of us is not that our aim is too high and we miss it, but that it is too low and we reach it.

~ Michelangelo

In the study of theology, there are two words that reflect theory and practice: orthodoxy and orthopraxy. The first is correct belief, and the second is correct practice; they are a working duo, like faith and works.

Knowing the *what* and *why* of our faith helps us to understand theoretically, but they do not automatically instill *how* to apply that knowledge in everyday life. While some of the how-to questions were addressed above, this section expands on practical ways to achieve spiritual goals. The following suggestions are just that: suggestions. They are based upon my experience, so take them for what they may be worth to you. Sometimes, we learn from the mistakes of others, and at other times, we must learn from our own. While the former is better than the latter, the important thing is that we learn!

A. Refocus How To Process Sound and Image.

Already mentioned above, our minds are influenced by the world around us, for better and for worse. We are inundated with harmful sights and sounds both real and virtual. Some are involuntary, yet others we invite. From films and television to music and the internet, our mind is bombarded with both positive and negative data. But unlike a hard drive that can be wiped "clean," we are stuck with the input. This is why an informed faith put into action provides a spiritual filter. A filter that allows in the good and keeps out the bad. Regarding the good, that we should freely allow to enter, we read about in Philippians Chapter 4, where the apostle Paul encouraged Christians to think about things that are:

true,
honest,

Chapter Five: Applied Theory or Practical Tips

just,
pure,

lovely,
of good
report.

By allowing virtuous input, we are positively feeding our new nature. Likewise, we have the challenge of filtering out the negative; and that may take some practice. Does being a news addict cause you distress? Start cutting back on your intake. Are you tempted to watch a questionable movie? Pause and think, "Would I want Jesus or Mary sitting next to me?" You get the picture.

God has created the most beautiful sights and sounds for the benefit of our senses, not to mention our peace of mind. Indulge in the profound diversity of nature. Scan the sky, watch a bird in flight, or listen to the sound of running water (I have two fountains). God has provided ample ways to positively input the good.

B. Avoid the Appearance of Sin.

The Old Testament rule regarding actual sin was expanded further by Jesus to include intellectual sin, where just a thought can be sinful. Another way to proactively protect our new nature is to avoid the appearance of sin. In other words, if a venue looks like a place Jesus would not enter—run! Invited to a party that may have drug use or alcohol abuse—run! We should flee from any person, place, or thing that might tempt us to sin. Running is literally what Joseph did.

Joseph, son of Jacob, ran from sin. When he was sold into slavery by his brothers and ended up a slave in the house of a high-ranking Egyptian official named Potiphar, Joseph was sexually tempted. Young and good looking, he caught the eye of Potiphar's wife. When Potiphar was not around, she began sexually harassing Joseph. He could have given in, but he refused her. And not only that, he reminded her she was Potiphar's wife and it would be a grave sin in the eyes of God. She persisted, and one day, when the two were alone in the house, she grabbed at his garment at which point he ran straight out of the house!

C. Physical Distancing.

When I came back to God's narrow path, the first action I took to avoid temptation was to stop dating. If I was not seeking marriage, I had no business socializing one-on-one. For me it was easy, yet one might say, "But I like spending time with him or her;" which is understandable, yet potentially problematic. First, it may crack the door that leads to temptation, especially if you are attracted to them (or they to you). Second, and in conjunction with the first, "But I like…" borders on selfishness that could hurt the other person's feelings down the road. This was a lesson I learned the hard way.

My best friend from church attended the same college as I did, and during the fall of our junior year, he declared his more-than-a-friend love for me. It caught me off guard. I loved him dearly, yet as the saying goes, "as a friend." Naively thinking that a heartfelt discussion would clear the air and allow us to resume our best-buddy routine, I was blindsided again when he said we could no longer be friends. Caught up in my own pain, it only occurred to me later that he had to distance himself to protect his own heart. All too often our perspective is one-sided, yet with a personal relationship, there are always two sides that need to be taken into account.

D. Mental Distancing.

Sacred Scripture teaches us that sin begins internally. Yes, we may first involuntarily see or hear or think something, but it is what we do at that point that determines sin or not. My dad used to say, "You can't stop a bird from flying over your head, but you can stop it from building a nest." That phrase has always stuck with me and encourages me to act immediately when my new nature is in danger of sinning.

My struggle has always been with music. I may not remember what I had for lunch yesterday, but if I hear a song from the 1980s or 1990s, I can tell you with whom I was in a relationship. Music triggers memories, often fond, yet spiritually dangerous. By simply listening to the radio, a song will transport me back in time to a person and place, and if I do not change mental gears (and channels) quickly, it may lead me to recall what is better forgotten. To be reminded of an intimate relationship, especially one that was happy, is going to occur. How far we take that memory is up to us.

> ### *A Note Regarding Past Relationships*
>
> *Cutting the ties to past relationships can be challenging, yet sometimes necessary. Years after my return to the Lord, one of my former boyfriends contacted me. It was nice to hear he was doing well, but I told him – politely - that I was not interested in staying in touch. For me, it was spiritually beneficial to distance myself from him, and the love I once felt for him, to maintain the integrity of my faith.*

E. Support and Accountability.

Being single does not mean we must be alone; just selective when it comes to companionship. We are social creatures who thrive on human contact, including family and friends. One of the best ways that I have found to keep focused on what is pure is to surround myself with good Christian friends. Having a friend that is equally devoted to the faith adds another spiritual guardrail to keep us on track. Looking back, it seems that God had a hand in constructing a guardrail by using my mother.

Not long after my father died, I asked my mom to move in with me. That's not everyone's cup of tea, but it worked for us. Having a best friend who was also dedicated to the precepts of God, living with me, added an extra safety net against temptation.

F. In the Word, not the World

The Bible is the number one selling book in the world, but it is probably the least read. The Old and New Testaments, written for our edification and instruction, gather too much dust. Sacred Scripture is more than just a collection of historical books and letters; it is inspired by God for humanity, and it is very much alive. The Bible is poetry, song, and the history of salvation. It is not meant to simply be read, but to be studied. The apostle Paul, in writing to his young protégé Timothy, said,

> All scripture is given by inspiration of God, and is profitable for doctrine, for reproof, for correction, for instruction in righteousness, that the man of God may be perfect, completely equipped for all good works.

Sacred Scripture has been called God's love letter to humanity and a guide to living. If someone you loved, who also loved you, wrote you a letter, how many times would you read it?

I recall a cradle-Catholic (confirmed pre-Vatican II) saying to me one day after reading my first book, "Baptists study the scripture a lot, don't they?" Then she added, "Growing up Catholic, we learned more about the Church and Tradition, than we did about scripture." It is true that Baptists study scripture, intensely (though most are ignorant of Church History), yet it is also true, and particularly since Vatican II, that the Catholic Church has emphasized the personal study of scripture. In America, for example, the USCCB daily publishes scripture from the Old and New Testaments for our edification. And Jesus himself told us to "Search the scriptures!"[22] The benefits to digesting and even memorizing sacred text are manifold. For example,

- *It calms us in times of trouble* (Psalms 23).
- *It lights our way in the path of life* (Psalms 119:105).
- *It reminds us we are loved* (John 3:16).
- *It increases our faith* (Romans 10:17).

---

[22] John 5:39.

One of the first verses I memorized as a child, encouraged by my parents, was Proverbs 3:5-6: *Trust in the Lord with all your heart, and lean not on your own understanding. Acknowledge him in all your ways and he will direct your path.* I cannot express how often this has come to my mind in times of stress!

Chapter Six

Speaking of Loneliness

Loneliness is being alone and resisting it. Solitude is being alone and embracing it as the beautiful place of encountering God.

~ Bishop Donald Hying

If you are a fan of classic rock music, you may be familiar with Harry Nilsson's Hit, "One," made famous by *Three Dog Night* in 1969. The first verse goes like this:

One is the loneliest number that you'll ever do
Two can be as bad as one
It's the loneliest number since the number one.

A few years later, Gilbert O'Sullivan released his hit "Alone Again (Naturally)" in which he sings of a suicidal lover left at the wedding altar, who in despair even alludes mournfully to God in the verse:

Leaving me to doubt
Talk about, God in His mercy
Oh, if he really does exist
Why did he desert me

Lyricists are poets with their words set to music. Throughout history they have provided ample fuel for love songs that reflect both joy and heartbreak, and in so doing, tend to represent being single as something undesirable. For example, both Frank Sinatra and Dean Martin sang, "You're nobody till somebody loves you." Being single, however, does not mean one has to be alone, or unloved, yet it may lead to an unwanted feeling of isolation.

The metaphorical "broken heart" is rarely fatal physically, yet the feeling of isolation should be taken seriously. Prolonged loneliness may lead to real issues of anxiety, depression, and even thoughts of suicide. Marcel LeJuene, President and Founder of *Catholic Missionary Disciples*, wrote a poignant article entitled "The Quiet Epidemic of Lonely People," and in that article he shared several experiences of Catholics suffering from an epidemic of loneliness. From the youth who flies from one sexual encounter to another, afraid that a real relationship will break their

Chapter Six: Speaking of Loneliness

heart, to the elderly who feel forgotten, no one is immune to the sense of isolation. And for those who struggle right now at this level, there is no shame in asking for help. God does not want anyone to ever feel isolated.

If I were to ask you to name the first isolated person in recorded history, would you answer "Adam." If so, you would be correct. One might think that Adam had no excuse to feel lonely. He was surrounded by the most magnificent plants and animals, in a perfect climate where he needed no socks or shoes, and had his Creator/God as his walking companion. It was literally paradise, and yet Adam did not see it that way. Of all the creation he saw, and animals he named, he did not find a similar counterpart for himself. Paradise, for Adam, began when God formed a woman from his own body. Then, Adam exclaimed, "This is it! She is part of me!" Eve was the answer for Adam's isolation.

I like to joke with God that had he created me in that perfect garden, there would be no humanity.

Surround me with flowers, trees, furry animals, and a perfect climate, and I am a happy camper. Add God, a library, and a dog, and it would indeed be paradise. Yet even while this is true, I too am not immune to feelings of loneliness, and this is why I will share a short list of personal suggestions. Take them for what they are, but I hope at least one helps you as it has me.

Building Friendships

Jesus told his disciples that there is no greater proof of friendship than for a person to die for another. Indeed, Jesus, who has called us his friend, did just that. Most of us will not have to die for our friends, but it is good to understand the reality behind the sacrifice. A real friend is someone who loves you for you. Like a mirror, they reflect your happiness and sadness. You laugh, they laugh with you. You cry, they cry with you. A true friend will "have your back" and yet not withhold confronting you about something detrimental. For me, other than Jesus, my parents were my truest friends, for no matter how far apart we lived, we were there for each other. Moving around for most of my life, however, meant retaining

Chapter Six: Speaking of Loneliness

few other friendships. Logistically, long distances dilute what was once next door.

When I was ready to retire, I wanted to downsize and leave the big city. Craving a slower pace of life, and with much prayer and research, the Lord guided me to a small town in a completely new state. Moving to a new place was nothing new, but relocating to a place where I knew absolutely no one would be a first for me and put my people skills to the test. Small town vibe is nothing like that of a large city, and I mistakenly thought it would be easier to get to know people. What I learned, however, was that it is just as hard to be the only stranger in town as it is to be one in a million. Realizing this, the first thing I did was to register with my local parish and begin attending Sunday Mass. Ironically, that did not help much!

Recently converting to Roman Catholicism, I had come to know two dozen people through my RCIA class. It was instant fellowship as we gathered together every Sunday before Mass, and I just assumed the next parish would offer the same atmosphere, but I was wrong. I learned that Catholic worship is, generally speaking, less social than evangelical worship. Catholics arrive five minutes before the

Mass and scurry away immediately after, while Baptists tend to linger. In addition, Baptists gather 2-3 times during the week, including age-appropriate classes before worship, and weekly bible studies. These extra meetings present opportunities for newcomers to engage with people on a more personal basis. At my new church, however, I attended weekly Mass for months before anyone offered more than a smile and "Peace be with you." Still longing for Christian companionship, I turned to the Lord and asked him to help me find at least one good friend in my church. In the meantime, I did not sit completely still.

During those first few months, I endeavored to learn the names of people in town that I interacted with, like neighbors and local business people. It also helped that I had purchased a 130-year-old house just off main street where "so-and-so" had lived for fifty years. By associating me with that house, some conversational ice was broken, which also gave me a chance to share my "prayer and research" story. And just as small talk, staying busy, and the love of my dog helped me to feel less alone, God answered my prayer.

The Sunday before Christmas a woman came up and introduced herself; her name was Nancy. As we spoke, she spontaneously invited me over for Christmas Eve dinner, and on that cold sacred night God kindled a friendship. We talked for hours. Nancy was a widow, cradle-Catholic, and lifelong resident who had raised three children. Her frequent invitations for coffee would often include other ladies as she would say to me, "I want you to meet so-and-so." Basic tools had helped me avoid isolation, but it was an answer to prayer that provided me with a true friend. Thanks to Nancy's grace-in-action, not only did I find a kindred spirit, but I am unable to number the folks I have come to know in our community.

> Friendship is born at that moment when one person says to another, 'What! You too? I thought I was the only one.'
> ~ C.S. Lewis

Jesus was described as a man of "sorrows and acquainted with grief." He left his home in heaven to be raised by loving, but human parents. Growing up, and being God, must have made him feel different from others. As truly God, he could not be lonely, but as truly human he could desire companionship. When he was in the Garden of Gethsemane, grieving over his upcoming passion, Jesus asked his friends for companionship in prayer, but they fell asleep, so alone he prayed. And there were more "alone" moments to come. Alone, he was betrayed by Judas Iscariot. Alone, he was denied by Peter three times. And alone, he was unjustly beaten and crucified. Through all these alone moments, Jesus never complained. Yes, he was God, but as a perfect human he also showed us that he could *feel a desire for companionship*, but without self-pity.

Consider a Pet

There are good reasons why Americans house nearly 200 million pets, and one is *companionship*. Having a furry (or scaley) creature around is proven to boost a person's well-being. In their February 2018 newsletter, the National Institutes of Health published an article on "The Power of Pets: Health Benefits of Human-Animal Interaction," which mentions potentially real benefits to owning a pet. Physical benefits included a decrease in cortisol levels (a stress-related hormone) and lower blood pressure, while emotionally animals were shown to reduce loneliness and boost a person's mood. Caring for a pet has always helped me to focus on something other than myself. Even on the worst day, when my crazy little Shih Tzu comes running up to me, I cannot help but smile. Animals are loving and *funny*!

Maybe you prefer a cat, a bird, or even an iguana, the point remains the same; when living alone, a pet rock is not going to take the edge off a lonely moment. Can't have a pet for one reason or another? Visiting local animal shelters, or better yet, volunteering, is a great place for unconditional, if not slobbering, affection.

Increase (or Decrease) Activity

Another form of coping with loneliness is to get involved, or, paradoxically, *less* involved. Just as too little activity is harmful to our body and mind, too much can be equally harmful. *The key is balance*, and that can be difficult. Studies have concluded, especially among school-age children, that too much activity is detrimental to mental and physical well-being. The March 31, 2024, newsletter of the National Education Association included an article by Tim Walker entitled "Study: Too Many Enrichment Activities Harm Mental Health." The article mentions that in addition to normal home-work and bullying, too, many extracurricular activities increase stress and anxiety with children not getting enough "down time." Moderation means balance, and balance allows us to thrive in stable and unstable environments.

After too many years of all work and no play – demanded of my employer - I went to work for a company that practiced a work-life balance. Encouraged to actually "go home" hours before my normal quitting time, I didn't know what to do with these free evening hours, so I enrolled in a stained-glass class. In a short time, I realized that by focusing on just *one* thing I could actually blow out the cobwebs that multitasking spins in the brain! Eventually I was able to incorporate a program I named "30-30" which consisted of thirty minutes of exercise and 30 minutes of spiritual contemplation several times a week. What a difference it made in my mental, physical, and spiritual being!

Practice J.O.Y.

As a child I was taught the acronym J.O.Y. (**J**esus first, **O**thers second, and **Y**ourself last) as a way of prioritizing God's will for our attention. As a single woman climbing the corporate ladder, however, I spent years spelling joy backwards. Joy was misconstrued as personal satisfaction, yet real joy in this life comes by "putting what should be first, first, and last, last," as Yogi Berra might have famously stated it.

Focusing on ourselves is important, yet that self-focus should be counterbalanced by attending to the needs of others as well. Doing so not only fulfills Jesus' command to care for one another, but we also benefit from a greater and more objective understanding of those around us. From family and friends to complete strangers and abandoned animals, there is no lack of need where others are concerned.

Learn Contentment

As Christians, we are unlikely to experience the extreme ups and downs of the apostle Paul. Initially a brilliant and proud Pharisee, after his conversion this single man gave his life in humble servitude to Jesus Christ. He suffered innumerable hardships, both relationally and physically, and his dedication to the Gospel of Christ resulted in martyrdom, yet he found contentment throughout a difficult life. To the church at Philippi, he wrote (Phil 4:11-13):

> …for I have learned to be content regardless of my circumstances. I know how to live humbly, and I know how to abound. I am accustomed to any and every situation—to being filled and being hungry, to having plenty and having need. I can do all things through Christ who gives me strength.

Dwell on What God Thinks of YOU

Finally, and perhaps best of all, one way to manage those moments of isolation is to talk to the one who loves you more than life itself: God. When I said in the first chapter that it was as if God were deaf to my prayers, that was my perception, not reality. God heard me, but he works according to his will, and not a clock. Our heavenly Father does not sleep, or get tired, and has no need of a calendar or clock, which makes him always available, yet God is not on-demand, and that can be frustrating. Consider the following verses carefully and reflect on what God really thinks of you.

> **Matthew 10:29**, *Even a little sparrow, worth but half a penny, God is aware of when they die. How much more are YOU worth to him!*
>
> **John 3:16**, *For God so loved the world that he gave his only begotten son, that whoever (that's YOU) believes in him will not perish, but have eternal life.*
>
> **John 15:15**, *Jesus calls YOU, "a friend."*
>
> **John 1:12**, *God calls YOU, "his child."*

Ever mindful of his children, God is willing and able to provide guidance and comfort during your worst moments. When Jesus was living on earth, he was a comfort and guide to his disciples, but when he ascended into heaven, he made two promises to them and to you. First, he sent the Holy Spirit as the *Paraclete* (from the Greek παράκλητος that means, "one who is called to help or console"). Second, Jesus promised to "never leave you nor forsake you." With those two promises, you may boldly approach God - just like my father often did - and expect his help. For Hebrews 4:16 says, "Let us then approach God's throne of grace with confidence, so that we may receive mercy and find grace to help us in our time of need."

Chapter Seven

Addressing Your Specific Status

I have learned, in whatever state I am, to be content.

~ The Apostle Paul

In this chapter, I would like to briefly address the various states of being single and what God desires, and expects, of each. When you think about it, we single people make up a large portion of the Church. We are virgins and non-virgins, divorced and widowed, and within those categories there are some brothers and sisters who question (or not) their sexual orientation. We are all different and yet no matter how unique we may be, God has the same will for us. In seeing you and me, he is equally just and right in what he expects and has gone to great length to provide a perfect standard by which to live. Unlike human society, which is in a constant state of moral flux, as new creations in Christ we are now bound eternally to God and to each other through his body the Church. As part of the one, holy, Catholic, and apostolic family, we are called to live in humility according to God's will and no other. This may prove difficult, for it means not only turning away from this world's glossy, yet imperfect ideals, but also checking the egocentric portion of our self at the door, if not kick it to the curb.

Virgins

Human beings are born "chaste," that is to say sexually pure or what we also call "virgin." Representing purity, the word virgin is often used to describe olive oil, a clear mountain stream, and the finest of wool. When the virgin state is altered, say through contamination, it is considered impure and devalued as such. Purity is regarded highly in the marketing of consumer goods, and yet, ironically, this is no longer the case sexually speaking. In fact, moral virginity is often mocked in our society, where, once upon a time, it was highly esteemed - which only proves, once again, how fickle and inconsistent the human moral code is. God, on the other hand, is constant, and his will is that a sexual experience only occur after two virgins marry. By entering holy matrimony as virgins, the couple continue in a state of moral purity. But one might ask, "What's the big deal? People don't care about that these days." The simple answer is that, despite our overly permissive society, God desires for us to be holy as he is holy. Pre-marital sex does more than change our physical state; it degrades the body and scars the soul. Contemplate the words of the apostle Paul who wrote to the church in Corinth:

> But sexual sin is never right: our bodies were not made for that, but for the Lord, and the Lord wants to fill our bodies with himself. Don't you realize that your bodies are actually parts and members of Christ? So should I take part of Christ, and join him to a prostitute? Never! And don't you know that if a man joins himself to a prostitute, she becomes a part of him and he becomes a part of her? For God tells us in the Scripture that in his sight the two become one person. This is why I say to run from sexual sin.[23]

Sex before marriage, then as now, is neither harmless nor trivial, and virginity should be guarded

---

[23] I Corinthians 6.

closely until marriage when "two become as one." Our body is the dwelling place of the Holy Spirit, and as he has graciously made his home in us, we should strive to protect the body from sin.

If it had been up to Paul, all Christians would remain forever virgin (he was that charismatic on the topic), but he also knew such an ideal was unrealistic and marriage was a holy option. Yet, Paul did make some good points when it came to remaining single, something that John Paul II also indicated in *Familiaris Consortio*.[24] In comparing a dedicated virgin to a virgin who marries, Paul noted that the latter tends to be more "this world" oriented. For the one that marries is, and quite naturally so, more concerned with temporal things, like their spouse or physical appearance. This is not a sin, of course, but what Paul is pointing out is that a single dedicated person tends to have, at least potentially, more time to focus on the things of God.

For the virgin, the will of God is: be holy as I am holy.

---

[24] *Familiaris Consortio* or "The Role of the Christian Family in the Modern World" is an apostolic exhortation that will be quoted in the chapter below.

Non-virgins

I voluntarily forfeited my virginity in my twenties in an act of rebellion against God. Blaming him for making me "the way I was" made for an indulgent yet dishonest excuse for my behavior. In the beginning, it was a convenient way to circumnavigate my moral responsibility, and later on I simply became callous toward the truth. Two decades of rebellion will harden a heart and sear a conscience, and had it not been for a loving Father in heaven, I may well have continued in that state.

Although God is merciful and patient, and desires nothing but the best for his children, we are free to disobey, yet when we do, there are consequences. *What goes up must come down*, as the saying goes, and regardless of our free will, God does not simply abandon us to it. If he did, he would not be Love. And that love, made a reality through Jesus Christ, allowed for us to become the adopted sons and daughters of God. But that love came at a very high price. Regenerated in the waters of baptism, we are no longer our own but new creations in Christ, and we, quite literally, belong to him. As our eternal parent, God will eventually step in and correct us, and if he does not, scripture tells us then that we are not his children.[25] The author of the Book of Hebrews tells us that God is a Father who disciplines his children when necessary. In Chapter 12:6 we read, "For those the Lord loves he disciplines," and in 12:11 the author adds, "Now punishment is unpleasant and painful, yet afterward it yields training in righteousness." Parents reprimand children to correct improper behavior. Likewise, God corrects his children when they stray too far from his will. It may seem like he has a long leash of patience, so long, we may forget about it, yet he never loses hold of us. Furthermore, his patience is linked directly to his love, which we know is equated to obedience. Just as our love for him is manifested through voluntary obedience, when we sin, God wants us to voluntarily wake up, repent, and return to him. The sooner we do, the quicker our relationship with him is restored. I threw away twenty

---

[25] Hebrews 12:8 says, regarding the subject of correction, "If you are not disciplined—and everyone undergoes discipline—then you are not legitimate, not true sons and daughters at all."

years of my life that I can never get back, but I am thankful for every moment since my return.

After my correction, I referred to myself as the "prodigal" daughter, echoing the parable of the prodigal son that Jesus taught.[26] This son decided one day to leave home and asked his father for his inheritance. Going far away, he spent all his money on wine, women, and song, and when the money ran out the party stopped. After a famine struck the area, poor and desperate, he took a job slopping pigs (a Jewish taboo) and became so hungry he considered eating their food. Finally, he awoke from his sin, and realizing what he had done he resolved to go home in humility and ask forgiveness of his father. This parable, which symbolizes a broken relationship with God, teaches us several lessons regarding our free will.

Prior to committing his sin, the prodigal son had the choice to:

A) never leave home or,
B) turn back.

---

[26] The word *prodigal* is an old term for what we would call today "reckless."

While committing his sin he had the choice to;

C) return before the money ran out, or
D) return immediately after it was gone.

Yet, and unfortunately for him, he chose:

E) to feed pigs while his own stomach remained empty.

Only when face down in a pig trough did the young man finally wake up, repent, and go home. When we desire to stray, our Father would prefer we choose "A," and never leave home, but when we do, there are still opportunities to self-correct (B, C, and D). These indicate how long God is willing to wait before he steps in; he is giving us a chance to do the right thing before we too end with option E.

The desire to sin may be appealing, even exciting; that's why it is preceded by temptation. Temptation is subtle, smooth, and intriguing to our senses; if it were not, sin would be rare. It is the delicious candy coating on a poison pill, that once getting us addicted, never fully satisfies us but leaves us wanting *more*. Choosing sin hurts God, damages us, and breaks our relationship with him. And in the end, it leads only to death, for the Apostle James wrote that, when we are tempted away from God by our desires, "… after [the] desire has [been] conceived, it gives birth to sin; and sin, when it is full-grown, gives birth to death."[27]

For the non-virgin, the will of God is:
be holy as I am holy.

Divorced

Divorce is real, and all too common today even among Christians, yet the word does not exist in God's vocabulary. When God instituted Holy Matrimony, it was meant to last for life.

Holy Matrimony is a Sacrament that contractually binds a man and woman together, as Jesus said, "So they are no longer two, but one flesh. Therefore, what God has joined together, no human being must separate."[28] The ideal is his will for us. There are, however, a few reasons in Sacred Scripture where cessa-

---

[27] James 1:15.
[28] Matthew 19:6.

tion of a natural marriage followed by a sacramental marriage is allowed:

1. where the marriage is illicit in the first place (consider the Leviticus holiness codes to which Christ was referring in Matthew 5:32)
2. where two pagans have entered a natural marriage and one becomes a Christian while the other does not and both agree to leave (Pauline Privilege, 1 Corinthians 7:15-16), freeing the baptized person to enter into a sacramental marriage; and

Additionally, the Catholic Church provides a third reason from Chapter 10 of the book of Ezra where Jews were commanded to put away their pagan wives.

3. where the "Roman Pontiff can dissolve a *non-consummated* marriage between baptized persons or between a baptized party and a non-baptized party at the request of both parties or of one of them, even if the other party is unwilling." (Code of Canon Law Can. 1142)

In the case of a sacramental marriage where both parties have validly and licitly entered a covenant with God, there is no breaking of the covenant, and even the wronged spouse is to remain single and celibate, as the Apostle Paul wrote,

> Now, for those who are married I have a command, not just a suggestion. And it is not a command from me, for this is what the Lord himself has said: A wife must not leave her husband. But if she is separated from him, let her remain single or else go back to him. And the husband must not divorce his wife. (1 Corinthians 7:10)

Not an expert on canon law, I am aware there exist valid cases for the annulment of a marriage, which, as a recognition that no marriage existed in the first place, is not the same as a dissolution. On this topic, it is best to speak with a priest or specialist. The overriding point is that today, with civil no-fault divorce laws in effect, a legal divorce between two Catholics may not be avoidable. It is important to understand, however, that just because a human law says it is okay does not mean that God agrees.

One thing is for certain when it comes to divorce - God commands that those loosed from a civil marriage yet who are found by their Tribunal to be licitly and validly married continue in their sacramental marriage. This means they must remain single and chaste. It is a hard fact that when it comes to God's moral law there is, at times, a sense of unfairness, but what we see as unfair, God sees as a continued state of holiness.

Other than spousal separation through death, divorce is perhaps the most painful of personal experiences. It not only hurts the couple, but also negatively impacts friends and family, especially children. Divorce is not a victimless sin. When it does happen, realizing there is hope in a loving God – who longs to comfort a broken heart – is the first step in healing.

Further information on what the Church teaches regarding divorce may be found in the *Catechism of the Catholic Church* (1650-1651; 2382-2386).

For the divorced, the will of God is: be holy as I am holy.

Widowed

The widowed, the man or woman who has been separated from their spouse by death, is close to the heart of God. The subject matter is mentioned extensively in both the Old and New Testaments, often in conjunction with orphans. The widowed are due honor and assistance from the Church. They are under God's protection, yet they, too, have moral obligations.

Widows are Due Honor and Assistance

In Exodus 22:22-24 we find a passage that describes what we would call today, "crimes against humanity." Here God told the Jews, "You shall not afflict any widow, or fatherless child. If you afflict them in any way, and they cry unto me, I will certainly hear their cry." In the Book of James (1:27), the apostle states that "Pure religion and undefiled before God and the Father is this: to visit the fatherless and widows in their affliction, and to keep oneself unspotted from the world."

Widows are Under God's Protection

In Deuteronomy 10:18, we are told that: "He [God] executes the justice for the fatherless and widow." And in Psalms 68:5; "A father to the fatherless, and a judge [protector] of the widows, is God in his holy habitation."

Widows are Free to Marry, but…

A person who is widowed may remarry, with one caveat; they are restricted to marry one in the faith who is also eligible (i.e., one that has never married, or is also widowed). In 1 Corinthians 7:8, the apostle Paul says: "I say to the unmarried and widows, it is good for them if they abide even as I. But if they cannot have self-control, let them marry; for it is better to marry than to burn." And if they choose to marry, it must be with a fellow believer, for Paul also states in II Corinthians 6:14, "Do not be bound together with unbelievers; for what partnership has righteousness with lawlessness, or what fellowship has light with darkness?"

For the widowed, the will of God is: be holy as I am holy.

On Sexual Orientation

For Christians who are attracted to the same sex, or both, a life imitating Christ presents its own set of challenges, particularly in light of today's more accepting environment. It may make the task difficult, but certainly possible. Once again it comes down to choosing between one's self and God.

Growing up in California, same-sex attraction was neither overtly public nor hidden from view. It was an open secret. My university had a small Gay and Lesbian club, and everyone knew San Francisco, West Hollywood, and Long Beach had LGBTQ+ neighborhoods. Exploring one's sexuality in the 1980s was a private affair; at least it was for me. Staying well under the radar of public scrutiny, I understood, as did most, that one's status did not improve if what was private became public. My, how the times have changed!

Today, people fight for a seat on the LGBTQ+ bus, whether gay or not. A lifestyle that was once a societal taboo is now a *cause célèbre* around the globe in a push for recognition as normal. While the positive publicity has worked, it does not alter the mind of God, and when public policy contradicts God's moral code, his children need to remain on his side. This is not a case of Mommy said "yes" and Daddy said "no," for human authority is not equal to God's. God has entrusted his Church and his children with the responsibility of reflecting him to the world and not the other way around. If we side with the world against him, we become his enemy.

In addition to secular approval, it is an unfortunate fact that some so-called "Christians" have joined the world against God. They have concluded that Christianity has been in darkness for 2,000 years, and only just now seen the light. Twisting Sacred Scripture, by interpreting it in a "modern" context, their theology is not credible. It reflects human self-interest, above the interest of God. Calling God's moral codes outdated, they ironically assume the ever-present God must have an expiration date. And perhaps, worst of all, they have redefined love, calling it "love is love," when the truth is that "God is Love." It is the smart marketing of a subtle lie, but do not fall for it. These groups only serve to enable disobedience. By cloaking the Christian consciousness with a blanket of "self-esteem," they mislead the faithful and numb the conviction of the Holy Spirit. Of these enablers, scripture has warned us. In 2 Timothy 4:3-4, Paul wrote:

> For the time will come when people will not put up with sound doctrine. Instead, to suit their own desires, they will gather around them a great number of teachers to say what their itching ears want to hear. They will turn their ears away from the truth and turn aside to myths.

On Sexual Orientation,
the will of God is: be holy as I am holy.

For all the sections mentioned above, one thing is certain: God does not change. He is who he is—holy. And his precepts are relevant, not relative. God does not adapt to human society any more than to the climate. The choice for us is one of two; either love God by showing him through obedience, or choose to disobey. Whatever way is chosen, there will be eternal consequences.

Chapter Eight

Examples of Dedicated Single Persons

Virginity or celibacy for the sake of the Kingdom of God not only does not contradict the dignity of marriage but presupposes it and confirms it. The vocation to the chaste single life liberates the heart in a unique way, "so as to make it burn with greater love for God and all humanity."

~ St. John Paul II[29]

In the quote above, St. John Paul II is restating one of Paul's arguments referenced in in the chapter above. The idea of a dedicated single life is not subject to time or culture; it is as relevant today as it was during the time of the Apostles.

---

[29] *Familiaris Consortio, 1981.*

Some of the examples below are of people who lived a long time ago, but that makes no difference to us, for like us, they were all single followers of Jesus Christ subject to the same set of moral rules and challenges. Cultural circumstances may vary slightly, but the human heart has never changed. And all people, rich or poor, educated or not, find themselves at one point in their life single. It is not who, but how we accept that status that matters.

Below are some examples of various Dedicated Single Persons who made a difference, both to God and to others, while living a consecrated life. I hope that you may be inspired by at least one of them.

Joseph – Son of Jacob

In the Book of Genesis, we are introduced to Joseph, the son of Jacob and Rachael, whom we mentioned above. He was a special young man, gifted early by dreams from God, who was sold into slavery by his brothers. Throughout his many trials as a young single man, Joseph maintained his spiritual integrity and went on to do great things for God.

Joseph & Mary

The parents of Jesus were perfect examples of placing God before their own desires. Joseph and Mary were legally married. They were entitled to an intimate relationship, yet they abstained from one another. Mary, ever Virgin, gave birth to Jesus the Messiah, her one and only child. And Joseph knew exactly what he was getting into from the start. In all likelihood, and this is speculation, Joseph was accepting of the situation of abstinence, just as he had been of marrying the pregnant Mary after receiving the message from the angel. Joseph and Mary placed God before themselves.

Anna – The Widow

Captured in the Gospel of Luke is a little story about a widow named Anna. She takes up but three verses in the longest book of the New Testament, but she was important enough to be included. Anna was a prophetess and the daughter of Phanuel of the tribe of Asher. As a virgin she married, but her husband died just seven years later. She was undoubtedly young, perhaps only in her early twenties, but she never married again. She spent the rest of her life in the temple, serving God daily with prayer and fasting. When Jesus was presented as a baby in the temple, Anna was there. At the age of eighty-four, she, along with Simeon's adoration and prophecy, proclaimed the birth of Christ to all those who "looked for the redemption in Jerusalem." Anna could have legally remarried, but something in her kept her from doing so, and she chose to spend the rest of her life solely dedicated to God.

John The Baptist

One could say that John the Baptist, the forerunner of Jesus Christ, was born to be single. If Jesus had a spiritual twin, it would have been John. These two cousins were born under miraculous circumstances, both lived a life of service in obedience to a calling from God, and both died for that calling. Jesus and John were only a few months apart in their birth and were, by way of Mary and Elizabeth's relationship, cousins. Like Jesus, we know very little of John's life prior to his ministry, but we may surmise that he, like

Jesus, became spiritually aware at a young age what God desired from him.

Being the only child and a son at that, he would have been expected to carry on the family name. Custom would have dictated that he marry and raise a family of his own, yet he did quite the opposite. Not only did he never marry, but he took up the odd position of living in the desert alone. Peter had been a fisherman and Paul a tent maker, but we see no trade or occupation for John except in preparation for his short-lived ministry.

Paul – The Apostle

Paul never married. We do not know why he was unmarried prior to his conversion; it was certainly customary for men of his age and standing in the community. What we do know is that after his conversion there is no indication that he ever sought marriage. Paul, who was truly a unique personality and something of a bulldog, appears to have been one who found complete solace in simply working for the Lord. In this, he was tireless. There were many times that Paul suffered for his service. Scripture tells us he was frequently jailed, beaten, stoned and even shipwrecked! If that did not make a person think twice about settling down to a 'normal' life, what would?

Paul had a calling that he willingly accepted, and in doing so, left us an example of the importance of both chastity and dedication in the life of a Christian. Below is a short list of those not found in the bible, but recognized later by the Church. The reader may note that some are now called "Saint" by the Church, but bear in mind that when they lived, they were ordinary human beings who chose to live extraordinary lives for God.

Agatha (d. 250)

During the time of the Decian persecution of Christians, Agatha, who was born into a wealthy family of Sicily, refused the continual advances of a Roman Magistrate. Knowing she was a Christian, who had taken a vow of chastity, he offered to save her life in exchange for sex. When she still refused, he had her imprisoned and tortured. She was barely twenty years old when she died.

Joan of France (d. 1505)

Born into royalty, Joan's early life was fraught with misery. Forced into marriage at the tender age of twelve, she literally grew up supporting her husband in times of difficulty, only to have him divorce her when he became King of France. In spite of her grief, she forgave him and turned her life into one of serving Christ. As a single woman, she would go on to found a religious order, The Sisters of the Annunciation, which remains active today.

Kateri Tekakwitha (d. 1680)

An Algonquin-Mohawk Native American, Kateri converted to Catholicism in her late teens. Her conversion was not welcome by some Mohawks, yet her love for, and chaste commitment to, Jesus outweighed any criticism or isolation. She died around the age of twenty-four.

Marguerite d'Youville (d. 1771)

Called "mother of universal charity" by Pope St. John XXIII, Marguerite had an unhappy married life and was only twenty-nine when she became a widow. Instead of focusing on her own situation, she worked with the local poor, ultimately founding the Sisters of Charity.

Isidore Bakanja (d. 1909)

An African convert in the former Belgian Congo, Blessed Isidore was zealous to share his faith. When his Belgian employer told him to stop discussing it at work, he did not and was beaten with a whip embedded with nails. Within six months, he died from his infected wounds, yet with a rosary in hand and brown scapular under his scant clothing, he died praying for and forgiving his attacker.

Joseph Moscati (d. 1927)

The first modern physician to be canonized, this single man assisted in saving people in Naples from cholera. His life was dedicated to others, so much so that he died between seeing patients.

Carlo Acutis (d. 2006)

Carlo Acutis was a remarkable young man dedicated to the Holy Eucharist. Born to Catholic, but non-practicing parents, Carlos embraced the faith at an early age. Through his own initiative, he took a personal interest in the faith and was a little imitator of Christ. Computer literate, he developed a website dedicated to Eucharistic miracles and Marion apparitions around the world. Diagnosed with leukemia on October 1, 2006, he died just eleven days later, aged fifteen. His final words to his mother were, "Mom, don't be afraid. Since Jesus became a man, death has become the passage towards life, and we don't need to flee it. Let us prepare ourselves to experience something extraordinary in the eternal life."

And lastly...

Your Name Here (d. _____).

When the book of your life closes its final chapter, what will your story reflect?

Chapter Nine

It Accumulates in "The End"

Be who you were created to be,
and you will set the world on fire.

~ St. Catherine of Siena

The Achilles heel of human society is the prevailing sense of "fairness" which is, ironically, never truly fair. If the standard for what is fair is based upon subjective definition, what is fairness fluctuates. The Oxford Dictionary defines "fairness" as *impartial and just treatment or behavior without favoritism or discrimination,* which sounds nice theoretically, but when fairness is based exclusively on human reason, it cannot be put into practice. It becomes a subjective ideal, and this "what is fair to me" definition fails the Oxford entry.

When justice is firmly grounded, when it is utterly immutable, only then may we speak of what is genuinely fair and apply it to all peoples in all ages and places. This, however, only comes about if fairness, or what we also call justice, is based upon God's will. True equity may only prevail universally when the code is universally *absolute*. Without this condition, the Oxford definition may as well read, "Fairness: refer to Situational Ethics."

God is the only standard by which we, as his children, are to live. It really is that simple: obey or disobey. We may not like all of God's moral rules, but liking them is not a factor in his equation. God would prefer we love his precepts and obey from a willing heart immediately, yet even if we balk at first, but later repent and obey, he counts it as obeying his will.[30]

As a human being, I view free-will as both a blessing and a curse. It is a blessing to my new nature, and a curse to my old, and both will be held accountable to God. Scripture tells us clearly that one day we will all stand before God and account for our "thoughts, words, and deeds." This life you now live is just the beginning, yet it is the most critical time in your existence. Here and now is the opportunity to, as St. Catherine of Siena says, "go out there and be who you were created to be," and in doing so "set the world on fire!" There are no regrets for those who

---

[30] Matthew 21:28-31.

Chapter Nine: It Accumulates in "The End"

have lived and died in the faith—only for those who did not.

Praise to you Lord Jesus Christ. Lord God, Lamb of God, Son of the Father: You take away the sins of the world; have mercy on us. You take away the sins of the world; receive our prayer.

www.ingramcontent.com/pod-product-compliance
Lightning Source LLC
LaVergne TN
LVHW051846080426
835512LV00018B/3093